crumble

Randi McCreary

By Randi McCreary

a beautiful mess
sweet water horizon

Lulu Press

9 781387 546268

For j&j

I

how many times have

we whored the oxygen-

passing reason for rum

shape shifting depressed mouths into

first kisses/again

gagging

at the back of the

throat in a wallowing

echo

we dissemble

as moans.

ii

he treats me

like the vineyard

touching softly

picking the ripest parts

collecting the juice

stomping me at the center

leaving me crushed.

iii

i could hear the last of his goodbyes

fading like brittle stones cascading

on a cold, still lake

a residue of good intention

drifting like debris

a million little pieces

of loneliness sifting into

the longing of my soul.

iv

i am tumbling towards you

a heavy load of laundered

thoughts you won't unfold

v

we are breaking

the still of morning

backs

sweat

bread

promises

porcelain

bad

generational curses

up

out-

vi

you promised to save me a star

somewhere in the blackened night sky

that would be for my eyes only

an extension of the galaxy

secluded for me

but on some nights-

she hopes for meteor showers

and miraculous seconds of streaming light

just like me

and it makes me wise not

to wish upon

anything.

vii

i would exchange thoughts

with the ant beneath my feet

if it would give me all of the answers

as to why you make me feel as

small as he,

but then i might be perceived as

crazy….

for loving you.

viii

i can be

your summer solstice

love you like

the longest day

sticky hot

and sheets off

in the after

of a forever sun

i can beam beyond

the hours in the counting

i can linger-

cast my line

against your comfort

press my finger

to your mouth

and hush your doubts

ix

this is sacred

resting in the palm of my heart

like a faberge egg

wrapped in porcelain

covered in glass

and tilting off balance

because i have

started to give

anything and it

looks as though

it is beginning to crack

and fall

into the

everything

you once

said i was.

x

i'll beg you to go

and punish my heart for words

it mentioned too soon.

xi

it tastes funny on the tongue

this love

a sour jar of stubborn splashed

across my buds when

i try to speak it into existence

a preserving liquid

that spritz its way through my ducts

salty and stunned

as to how it got here

puckering my brain

into a pout of disbelief

that remind me

how something

as cool as a cucumber

could find itself

in such a pickle.

xi

i'm afraid of what it could be. could be hours before we're finished talking and the owner flips the sign to *closed.* could be ours but i'm *too* closed off from what it could be is what i've been for too long. too long, for you is a sacrifice i cannot make and i cannot make sense of even my thoughts without being afraid.

xii

yes, i'm going to be there

to whisper your name through the wall

that separates you from me

when you have forgotten it

and can no longer

think and wipe and bite and

swallow such a hard pill

as time taking all things away from you

so you rely on staring out a window

that lets in the rays of

a familiar sun

you swore you walked beneath

and you are right-

even though what's left

is just a memory.

xiii

we've built more fences

around our hearts than august

could have imagined.

xiv

i couldn't sleep.

worry does that-

maybe a bulging disc in my back

or a rare cancer of sorts eating away

 at the skirt of my spine.

it could be every sprinkle of tar

that made its way to my lungs from

inhaling toxic air and N\nostalgic nickel bags

and even seedlings crossed my mind when I knew afterall

that we were never safe just to feel close

and wouldn't that be

a miracle delayed

but as i shifted

my weight and sighed

towards the moonlight

it was just the labor of thought.

xv

i've never seen eyes

quite like yours that can see me

just as i should be.

xvi

i'm beautifully broken

into shattered pieces

no longer fitting together

round where once flat

frayed at the edge

just enough for a story to tell

i am a tragic treasure

fine china and bull-

shit i didn't want to face

that i'm ready to make up

a lonely place that is longing to be alone

for the first time in a lifetime of

whatif and waste

a delicate mistake bold enough to tear.

xvii

you've escaped me

brilliantly

by gas lighting your tongue

and

i

watched

like a lamb to the slaughter

so impressed with the fire

i only offered more water

for me to drown in.

xviii

love gave me lemons

yellow in their citrus glory

squeezing the zest

out of me if i tried to escape

popping a seed in my eye

and blinding me from logical reasoning

if my back bone tried to sprout and grow

they seemed to know-

like little telepathic rinds

that read my mind...

what was i thinking?

xix

i keep thinking someday-

i'm going to run off with yasiin bey and we'll buy a catalog of funk and groove

that put us in the mood to share thoughts and ink

we'll leave our dishes in the sink so we can slow dance in the living room to thelonious monk

get sunk on lena horne and paint a plethora of canvas in nothing but green

wear berets just for the fuck of it

speak brilliant artistry like jean and josephine

i'll shatter plates on the floor. break them like bread just for that rebellious feeling

kiss him hard so he floats to the ceiling as if poppins

mary

my life will be our song

it will be a stunning hell of a romance that sets us free

but until then-

it's just me.

xx

i'd wait up for you-

if that's what it took.

greet you in nothing but my wu-tang

shirt if that had you shook

let you climb the walls and paint them

one layer at a time

if that's the motion that you'd second

just so i'd be first in line

deep down knowing that's just not me

i'd rather read a book and sleep

memorize the lines in your palm without making a peep

not even a whisper…

but i often wonder if you've kissed her

pulled the back of her hair like it was mine and dissed her

just enough to keep her jealous and wondering

what we do.

xxi

let the feelings

fall like bouquets of

pink chrysanthemums

the word

when they ask what we are

we'll give them

nothing

so we can

save it all for us.

xxii

what good

is gravity

when the kiss suspends me

the soft touch ends

me

freely

into a vanilla sky

where i have it all

mastered

to fall

xxiii

i searched for myself

in the pitch- black dark

of night

under mattresses

and wrinkled sheets

on a dampened waiting corner

of busy streets

inside of luke- warm cups of

tummy taming tea

within the pages

of brewing sonnets written

to set me free

alongside curbsides

for sobbing

and between the

syncopated

spaces of indulgent throbbing

where i came for you

i used to love

the way your weight felt against me

someone you could lean on

your hands

heavy as the summer rain

a weightless balance

that left me beaming

but it was

never a trust

fall at all

when i knew

you were just

pushing me away.

xxiv

i've taken a vow of silence

for my heart

keeping it muted

against all odds

covering its urge to shout out love to the mountaintops

with my quivering hand

i muffle the beat

with my pleading

maintain a ghostly hush in the hopes you will not hear

the stream of it bleeding

i have mastered the art

of being jaded

but staying faded in the corner of an emotional ball

glitter, glitz and a stumbling fall

that i hope never startle you

xxv

you cupped the sides

of my hips

like you were holding

heaven in place

xxvi

you have been checked out

like library books on shelves

i cannot read you.

xxvii

our love was grand

like a piano. in tune.

until it went flat.

xxviii

i would have loved you

anyway that i could have

loved you anyway.

xxix

i

fell into

love

just for a moment

just the tip

just because

just while no one is looking

just trust me

just let him

just hurry up

just finish

just don't say anything

just go

just in case

just remember

it isn't love.

xxx

we tend to pick fights

then share the very last bite

of forever.

xxxi

i used to laugh through the pain

until it hurt to laugh

and belly aches caused

tear gas

so i lay low

under covers

and lie.

xxxii

he used to tell me

only onions made him cry

so i left the ring.

xxxiii

feed my soul a phat girl's diet of porridge and praise

wrap a bib around my neck before you serve me the truth

pour me a tall glass of i can't live without you

and make sure it's on ice

serve it to me twice with a side of good intention

make me a gravy out of kneaded promises

like fussed over gnocchi

put in my face a giant bowl

of intellectual poke

garnished with a joke that only i know

show me the garden in your backyard

where the lies grow

and let me help you weed it

pass me the butter me up

because you know i need it

i am hungry

so give me takeout and take me in

i want to be drunk off of your kisses

like they're a bottle of spiced tamarind gin

and i'm swaying in the booth

say something sweet because you know my sweet tooth

smuggle me loaves of indiscretion

from your local spirit

keep the pantry filled with your loving arms and discard

all the needless harm because we don't need it

feed it slowly

let the extra drip down my mouth because

love is hard to swallow

xxxiv

i've got you

like

pennies and lent

snug tight

in the back

pocket

that no one

tends to

think of

until they

need change.

xxxv

they say when it is you

i will know -

just as the water knows

the tide will take it

xxxvi

you treated me

feather light

in the heavy times

spun a web of

sanctuary around

my fret and dipped the sharpest

edge in gold-

you made me rich with solace

sent me

baby butterflies

to host

and the flutters

are a waltz

i want to dance.

xxxvii

i seem to be pro- longing

i believe in the drear

and hope the worst will be champion

i protest the descent

and march for the breakup

ignore the soothe and haunt the shakeup

there is something wrong with me

that is the song of me

always performed solo

so i can go

on and and on and on

about

how no one cared.

xxxviii

i have seen walls-

watched boulders broken down

just to form a structured barrier

i have

leaned against

slabs of sturdy concrete

and curled my fingers through

the holes of a gripping iron

fence

still knowing no

hurdle exists

that could keep me from you.

xxxix

i think we met again-

gazing at the honest place in one another

that we thought was lost

we spoke a new language

coating the assumptions

in a new polished way of patience

i think i recognized you

just for a moment

passing you in the daytime

wishing it was night

so i could hold you

tender as the day

safely as your secrets

that i still lock away.

xl

i could touch my own heart

if i tried

reach into a concave

where

certainty used to be

feel the cold

insulate the obsolete

one step at a time

and be renewed.

xli

you are the perfect

pecan for my daydreams

sweet and tempting

like august naps

and perhaps

this is what it means

to be spent

the universe i

can't resent-

for sending you to me

in perfect form

let's make this

the norm

and call it forever

xlii

i'm convinced

this is an elevator romance

pressing my buttons

filled with awkward silence

and blank stares

going downhill

in a small space

with the hopes

that a new

door will open.

xliii

he serenades me slow songs

of let's get you home

cupping my shoulder blade

with the good intention of

shoving me into what

he can flag down the fastest

a parted window.

a drooping head on his chest while

the meter ticks us

to the side of

a brick building i won't recall

we press lips quick and darted

like strange birds pecking at the

same seed and my wings are broken.

xliv

i've taken up sewing

since i last saw you.

threading a scowl across my face

and knitting a line or two

to match my brow

i fill a thimble with

spools of tears

and try to hang on like

the yarn that denies the thread

i have fashioned

myself a heavy quilt

of shame to keep

me warm and think that maybe-

nothing else will unravel.

xlv

keep the soft thoughts

tucked away under your temple

and i won't tell the world

let them see you cut against the air

with your eyes straight ahead

and only i will know they

often close to rest

make believe the iron fist is callous

when i have held your

tender hand

xlvi

the plenty of fish

that there were supposed to be

never swam to me.

xlvii

i may have to

bare

down

and give birth to our ending.

grit my teeth

and break the cycle

of forgiving it all

a labor of longing

that i do not want to

crown

but i am fatigued

from not showing

my best self.

i warned him a poem would come of this-

that a couplet could arise

when I'm aroused from every kiss

i alerted him that

touching my figure

could become figurative

love making on linoleum the anaphora

i could not

floor-

lust personified

a tree squeezing the reason

out of the

thickness of my thigh

i advised him not to

punctuate the urge-

period.

xlix

wish he thought of me

like that of the bumblebee-

someone to die for

l

he misses the

mornings where we would

break/fast-

scraping toast to make it look

as if he hadn't burned me

scrambling eggs like excuses

beaten and hurt

so now i only

crave

dessert

li

my fingertips

tingling and tempted

to take each word

that trickles from your lips

pick them one by one

like

wild plums

that have

grown a

prickly thorn

and

dispose

the point

of it

all

lii

the moon

looks small from where we watch

wrapped in our favorite blanket

sharing a piece of peace

and relishing in bets of how

we would find a way

to get there

i'd walk

you'd run

we'd meet

somewhere in between-

out of breath and shaking off stardust

that looked much

like your smile

liii

harvest me in your arms

nibble me up

like blackberries

       full

pick me over time

and move the

earth

liv

when you give

me your word

put in just the tip-

let the w slip

in slowly until

the o

feels right

let me get used

to the r

when the d makes it feel tight

because

the truth

hurts.

lv

failure

swarms around us

a

nocturnal firefly

lighting our trust up in flames we cannot temper

forgetting how the

water works

we choose wine

and let it all burn.

lvi

i'm healing on

mahogany where

we slept

my ears ache from silence

no patterned breathe and restlessness

i am hollow against the air

no arms to hold my weight,

no hips to rest

my weight

my worries

and morning seems a place i cannot

dream towards fast enough

lvii

thank you for

the lemonade

three ice cubes and freshly squeezed

poured long

aside my thoughts

on the day

you left

and

this is what's refreshing

lviii

just for a moment

i toyed with the thought of leaving

but then i remembered that you never liked a mess

and loss is never tidy so i brushed

the thoughts to the edge and watched

them fall fast like ashes

that i knew i would have to

clean up before you noticed

lix

you are housed

exquisite

in my brain

living in the

grand suite of my cerebrum

hanging self-portraits

from my frontal lobe

that leave me speechless

and i know

there's

nothing left

lx

brown as butter

soft like sugar on my tongue

i crave melanin

lxi

watching you sleep

wondering

behind the fluttering of eyes

if i came to you in a dream

if we solved it all peacefully

on a deserted beach of crystal sand and seagull

if you saw me again in a light renewed

or were you just lying

awake

behind tired lids

too afraid to

face me.

lxii

i cut the stems at an angle

and hope they will last

fearing like us

they will be quick to die fast

the vase protects their purpose

but you and i

divide no glass

and often break

lxiii

you adore

the dark cloud in me

a cumulus attraction that says your

in it for the long fall

lxiv

there is a page missing

with words i haven't mentioned

a painful alibi for why my ink runs dry

just a grueling lyric to dance to

but playing on repeat when i have asked it to stop

this line is a tragedy

and this one a declarative blues

they only cease

when i do

lxv

my blues is turning violet

now that you have stroked it

with a brush of kindness

the lioness

in me has begun to purr

i've shed a layer of satin from the fur

and feel that i am royalty

foolish of me never to consider this hue

that you have glazed and dabbed

until the canvas bleeds away the blue and turns

violet

violet

violet you're turning violet ,violet

and

isn't it melancholy to mauve

when the cobalt is through.

lxvi

the car almost got sold today. the buyer asked if we could
down the price

because there were stains on the rooftop, but he doesn't know
that's from wine being doused on

my head while we drove. or why there's a crack in the
window from my forehead being sturdier

than i had imagined. and it never rolled up quite the same
after a backhand from the backseat

sent your favorite cap flying. the carpet flooring insecure
because you chose to conceal without

me knowing. and i'd never been more terrified to drive. is that
hail damage, or did she vandalize

the side again when she learned you had me waiting at home
or nursing the sidewalk wondering

what my keys felt like going in the ignition. it was foreign to
me.

the car almost got sold today but i turned it down so i'd never
forget why i should never

go back down that road.

lxvii

chances are you read this years ago-

       across my face where the wrinkle offsets my frown

in the faint lines of my hand that don't reach for you

in the silence

in the shuddering sigh

on the wall where portraits of us came down

atop the cold space on the mattress that has demented warmth

in the thick tension of humid air

  there was always a language

you never mastered

lxviii

making love to you

and still conquering the day

is called bone structure

lxix

i'm trying to

wean

from the lust that sent me

wet

and

loose

like pasta tested against the wall

it never fails

i love them all.

the bridge of his nose.

cologne and stiff cognac.

the martinis are so dirty.

faint scent of defeat

the saddle and whip

if i could just stop biting his bottom lip

and suck it up.

lxx

we avoided the mess

with

sandwiches wrapped thin in parchment

chewing slowly to get to sunset

without having to bring up the truth

we'd split cokes and baby ruth

in an empty theater that mirrored our sadness in pixels

and dread the ending

because pretending could last a little longer

i guess we both could have been a little stronger

but I prefer my knees weak

enough that i can't pick up the spills

lxxi

he likes me plunged in promises

and draped in loyalty

spinning in a pearl spun necklace

of royalty

it is glamorous

a sweet pan chocolat

cascading tiara of pulled hair in knots

from the window

yes-

hips become song

until the curtain is closed

and he tells me

i'm wrong

lxxii

stretch the night across my shoulders

and brush my hair with evening air

gift my ankles jewels of sand

and play me an orchestra of oceans

bend the branches so they'll bow to me

bottle up the galaxy

and pour me its perfume

lxxiii

i can't look at you

without seeing what went wrong

when you looked at me

lxxiv

never is your girl-

she mounts on second thoughts

to slowly ride you to the climax

of obscurity

and tempts you

with the prospect of absolutely

nothing that i can do

about it

lxxv

i was washed in the scent of you in winter

a wool sweater for crosswords puzzles

sage and cinnamon behind my ear

mint and honey for your tea

we shared dull pencils

and poor guesses

looking for four letter words for love-

boxing ourselves in and not realizing

it was

over

lxxvi

i can't imagine

if not your sanctuary

what i will become

lxxvii

i am

naked

with my heart exposed

a wandering emperor with no clothes

bare enough to know

you won't cover me

lxxviii

peace finds me

my own beloved

under a weeping willow tree

humming acapella odes to the tune of free

i confess my self love

in broad daylight and piercing night

i am enough

lxxix

i'm afraid i've caused

the earth to drown

in my tears

that i've relied on the willows

to wipe my eyes

and sobbed too loud

i have thrown one stone too many at

calm rivers

and blamed the ripple on the wind

but this is just my nature

lxxx

we were falling as if snow

melting in silence

like flakes against the eager tongue

until the moon peaked under

the dance of a hundred stars.

love caught us heavy

like sacred words

spilled

in a silent blue room

an imperfect perfection of

streetcar kissing afternoons

we were soul and sangria madrid

swing dance on the vine

and you were mine

lxxxi

i want to die

      just a little today

it could be in your arms

at the elbow

or in the fleeting moment

before you would have said

goodbye

lxxxii

and what else/?

Routine.

Like everything was in its place.

Nothing out of order.

A silent house.

He used to press against me and whisper, *Let's watch the sun go down,* but now the sun was just a ball of gas ready to explode.

I could relate.

He used to walk in our home to the most wonderful smells. Aromas that woke up his spirit and made his stomach convince his heart that I was the woman he had always needed.

Smoke and music, spattering oils and spatulas. A spoonful of this or a pinch of that for tasting. *Too much salt* he'd warn, and so a bit of sugar would go in. A dab of cayenne. He was willing to taste anything. I still remember. I had a way of making him forget. A maroon tinted chutney would be scooped up by the finger and slipped between the tip of his lips. I would place a dab of hot mustard behind his ears. Nibble until the heat kicked in.

I used to make him hungry. For short ribs smothered in thick gravy. For smoked black eyes. For rich cobbler. For me. No peaches now. Just the dry forming of words and the bitter taste of distance. *We're out of paprika. Palm oil if there's time. We need plantains and parsnips. Parsley and persimmons.* And so, he'd rush out the door and return. I kept my head down and endured. Stewed and stirred. I'd pry his lips open and make him taste until his eyes would say-

And what else?"

Butterscotch

And what else?

Cardamom

And what else?

Breasts and thighs

Of course I'll kiss you there.

And what else?

It used to be our sacred banter that led to exhausted naps. We were everything you wish love is until you are in it. Swelling on our way to deflation like dough angry to rise.

lxxxiii

love can be the luscious pie that holds on to its humble

but

    we

    indulged

      in gluttony

and sadly

    watched

    it

c r   u m

    ble.

CPSIA information can be obtained
at www.ICGtesting.com
Printed in the USA
BVHW031227071122
651337BV00016B/435